Keeping It Simple

Keeping It Simple

The Do's and Don'ts
of Real Estate Investing

S.M Cullen

Copyright © 2014 by S.M Cullen.

Library of Congress Control Number: 2014907186
ISBN: Hardcover 978-1-4990-0120-4
Softcover 978-1-4990-0119-8
eBook 978-1-4990-0118-1

All rights reserved. No part of this book may be reproduced or transmitted in any form or by any means, electronic or mechanical, including photocopying, recording, or by any information storage and retrieval system, without permission in writing from the copyright owner.

Any people depicted in stock imagery provided by Thinkstock are models, and such images are being used for illustrative purposes only. Certain stock imagery © Thinkstock.

Rev. date: 06/25/2014

To order additional copies of this book, contact:
Xlibris LLC
1-800-455-039
www.Xlibris.com.au
Orders@Xlibris.com.au
620658

DISCLAIMER AND DISCLOSURE

This publication, including its attached material, is for information and instructional purposes only. The author makes no warranties or guarantees, express or implied, in relation to income from the material supplied.

The author is not a practising solicitor or certified accountant. This information is not designed to provide you with professional, legal, or taxation advice, and the author strongly recommends that you consult with your lawyer or tax accountant in relation to your real estate investment activity. It is your responsibility to comply with your local, state, and federal laws, rules, and regulations.

Every effort has been made to make this publication as accurate as possible; however, there may be typographical and/or content errors. Therefore, this book should serve as a guide only. This material may also contain information that may be dated.

The author and publisher shall have no liability or responsibility to any person or entity regarding any loss or damage incurred, or alleged to have incurred, directly or indirectly, by the information contained in this publication.

Any and all web sites referred to in this book are provided for informational purposes only and do not constitute endorsement for any products or services provided by these web sites, and the sites are subject to change, expire, or be redirected without notice.

This book is intended for the purchaser only. Reproduction of this publication is unlawful. The purchaser may not copy in part or whole any information in this book by means of print, video, audio, electronic, or other means without the written consent of the author.

Contents

Author's Note 1
Introduction 3

Don't! Negative Gear 5
Do! Short-Term Capital Growth 11
Don't! Be Afraid of Risk 19
Do! the Research 23
Do! Remember 'Caveat Emptor' 27
Don't! Under-Insure 33
Do! Create a Company 39
Don't! Avoid Your Taxes 45
Do! Keep Thorough Records 51
Don't! Use Only One Lender 55
Do! Pay the Professionals 59
Don't! Delay, Start Saving Now 61
Conclusion 65

Your Checklist 68
Index 71

For My Children

The single-most powerful asset we all have is our mind. If it is trained well, it can create enormous wealth in what seems to be an instant.

(Robert T. Kiyosaki, *Rich Dad, Poor Dad*)

AUTHOR'S NOTE

My decision to write this book was based on my husband and partner, John. John is a good man and he is very supportive in our business ventures, but his inability to retain interest in a 300-page book about investing in real estate proved to me that there was a real need for 'keeping it simple'. I didn't want this book to be painfully repetitive or write it so that it was 'filled with fluff', for want of a better term.

Don't get me wrong. John is an extremely intelligent man; he just doesn't have the time or the patience to indulge in a 'novel' to get to the key points. My goal in writing this book is to keep it brief as well as simple, while providing you with the key points, then allowing you to spend further time in understanding and implementing them should you decide that investing in real estate is for you.

So to keep this as brief as I intend to keep the book, I have simply outlined the most important elements for you to understand the *dos and don'ts* of real estate investing while keeping it *'John-Easy'* to read, as well as inspire you to invest your time, your mind, and your future in real estate.

I hope you benefit greatly from reading this book and wish you well on your journey to attaining financial freedom through real estate investment.

INTRODUCTION

Whether this book is your first financial investment towards your future in the property market or whether you are a seasoned investor, this guide is intended to assist you in attaining your goals, protecting your assets, increasing your knowledge, and growing your property portfolio effectively and efficiently.

Before I begin, first and foremost, I would like you to understand the word 'equity' and what it means, because it is just not a very commonly understood word in relation to real estate. Equity is a very important consideration for where you are now in the investing game and where you intend to be with your real estate investing. Particularly, if you have been pondering the idea of purchasing your first investment property for some time now and had absolutely no idea that you could have been using the equity in your own home to get you started.

Equity in real estate is defined in the *Oxford Dictionary* as 'The value of a mortgaged property after deduction of charges against it', which basically means *that it is the difference between* the value of the property and the amount financed on the property. So if you have a property that is valued at $450,000, and your mortgage on that property is $300,000, you have an equity amount of $150,000. You can use that $150,000 as a deposit (or leverage) for your first or your next investment property.

Equity in your properties is an asset, *your* asset. If you have it, it's time to start using that equity effectively in order to make you money. It can get you through the first step of investing in the property market, and it can help you continue to grow your portfolio, your wealth, and your assets.

That is why equity is the main thing that I want you to be aware of as you read through this book. It affects your borrowing power and your property portfolio. It will also help you clearly assess whether you have a good deal on your next property purchase or not. You will become aware of the strategies that you can use to increase the value of your real estate and thereby *create* more equity in your properties. As I run you through the property investment guidelines, I ask that you keep the word 'equity' in the back of your mind.

Without further ado, let's look at the *dos and don'ts* of real estate investing.

Chapter 1

DON'T! NEGATIVE GEAR

Negative gearing is a dying trend. You would be surprised at how many times I've been told that negative gearing is 'definitely, no ifs, buts, or maybes the way to go', and I have disagreed on almost every occasion. Mainly because, nowadays, there is a large amount of property available on the market that is positively geared, so it makes very little sense to me to invest in a negatively geared property. Now, if there was no possible way of getting your hands on a property that gives you an income, then (and *only* then), I would agree with this claim; because a negatively geared property sitting in your portfolio is still better than *no* property sitting in your portfolio.

In my view, though, the personal income tax benefits of a negatively geared property are not enough to convince me that anyone should have a property in their portfolio that is costing them money. As soon as a property is costing you money, it is no longer an asset to you; rather it has become a liability.

There is obviously something to be said for negative gearing; after all, a significant number of property investors worldwide are doing it. But it's just not for me. I want my real estate assets to pay for themselves; I do not want one cent of my personal income spent on a property. I could probably even deal with breaking even, where both the costs of owning the property and the income of a property are of the same value, but actually having money (or a passive income) coming into my bank account wins hands down.

Okay, so what is all this negative gearing versus positive gearing all about in layman terms? Simple . . .

> *Negative Gearing = costing you money*
>
> *Positive Gearing = making you money*

Negative gearing is basically where there is a shortfall between the rental income that you receive from the property and the costs associated with owning the property. That means that you will have to find cash from your personal income to make up for the shortfall.

The income that you can generally make from a negatively geared property will be when the real estate market rises in value over time. If you want immediate incomes that you are not physically working for, then aim to have *all* your investment properties positively geared.

A positively geared property will not only pay off the mortgage that you have on it, but it will also give you extra cash to play with or invest in your next property. With negatively geared property, you will still gain long-term profit by the increase in the property's value over time, but positively geared real estate will pay for itself from the outset while also creating a passive income for you. You would be surprised at how quickly a few positively geared properties can boost your personal income.

How do you make sure that you are investing in a positively geared property and not a negatively geared one? Well, what I am about to say is not technically the correct way to calculate whether you have a negatively geared or a positively geared property in your portfolio because there are so many calculations involved. I am certain that I will probably get a few slaps on the wrist from many astute investors for even suggesting it, but it's fast, it's effective, it's simple, and it works for me. So what the hey? I'll tell you anyway—the easiest way for you to figure out whether it is a positively geared property is by going online and finding an *interest only* mortgage calculator. By entering the relevant details, including the loan amount, the percentage rate, and the term of the loan, the mortgage calculator will tell you what your weekly repayments will be. If the average weekly market rent in that location, for a similar style property, is not even covering the weekly mortgage repayments, I would consider it a poor investment choice.

You will still achieve capital growth when the value of the property goes up in the years to come, and you may benefit when you lodge your income tax return at the end of the financial year, but in the meanwhile, you are out of pocket on a weekly, fortnightly, or monthly basis.

In other words, regardless of your deposit (the funds that you personally contributed to the purchase), if your loan amount is $250,000 at 5.9 per cent, then your weekly mortgage repayments would be about $283, and if the rental return that you can expect to achieve from that property is only $270 each week, you may think to yourself, 'Well that's only $13 more per week. I can afford that.' You may well be able to afford that, but that is not the issue—the issue is that a negatively geared property (a *liability*) is being added to your portfolio. It's not just '$13 more per week'; it's $676 per year, and over fifteen years, that's $10,140, that is coming directly out of your pocket to purchase this property, when you could have found a positively geared property that puts those dollars into your bank account, where it belongs.

Negative Gearing Example:

Mortgage Repayments ($250,000 @ 5.9%) = $283
Rental Return = $270

Loss = $13

Had you been aiming at finding a comparable property in a similar area where your mortgaged amount would have only been around $200,000, and not $250,000, your repayments would be approximately $226 per week, and with a weekly rental return of $270, it would be putting $44 each and every week into your bank account. That's $2,288 each year, or $34,320 over the fifteen years that's coming into your hands, not out.

> **Positive Gearing Example:**
>
> *Mortgage Repayments ($200,000 @ 5.9%) = $226*
> *Rental Return = $270*
>
> *Profit = $44*

This example is just the bare bones that demonstrate how you can easily find yourself negatively gearing a property, and the mortgage calculations are based on an interest-only loan. The reality is that you probably won't be holding on to the property for fifteen years, you may or may not decide to take out an interest-only loan, and rental prices can increase or decrease during this time.

There are also other expenses that I didn't mention such as acquisition costs, periods where your house sits vacant, and interest rate rises, but nor did I mention all the allowable tax deductions including council rates, repairs to the property, management fees, and depreciation. Phew! That's a lot, but I chose not to give you an extensive list of all these items because they generally offset each other; that is, those extra costs paid by you, more often than not, will be cancelled out by the taxation benefits, so they hold no significant relevance when it comes to calculating your mortgage repayments versus your rental income when you are looking at an investment property.

The purpose of this book is to provide you with the bare essentials, and that includes encouraging you to make it your priority to ensure that your next property purchase is a positively geared one.

Negative gearing calculators are also available online for you to use and they will be a little more tailored to your specific circumstances. They will take into account your income, the area that you are purchasing in, your loan to value ratio, the tax benefits, and other details that are personalised to you. So take the time to do your figures here as well.

The negative gearing calculator (depending on the relevant information that you enter) may or may not tell you that my first example of a $250,000 mortgage while renting the property out at $270 per week is a negatively geared property. However, I am a little more sceptical on vacancy periods and unforeseen events. I prefer to *know* that my mortgage repayments are covered each week for the duration of the loan, rather than wait until the end of the financial year to see the tax benefits that have been generated by my property. Plus, it gives me a buffer for any future interest rate rises.

Ultimately, it's up to you whether you are seeking to supplement your loan repayments with a higher level of cash flow or whether you prefer to see out the financial year and benefit from the property's income at that time; in any case, please, please, please make sure that your investment property is positively geared regardless of how and when you choose to receive the income provided by your investment.

Accountants and tax specialists can tell you all the advantages of negative gearing; essentially it is to offset your personal yearly income taxes. I'm sure that it makes all the logical sense in the world to them, but in my opinion, it seems to be a very old-school train of thought that was generally targeted at an investor aiming to own one or two properties outside of the family home, while also working their full-time job. I assume that you are reading this book because you are different; *you* want a portfolio; *you* want to accumulate several properties and reap the rewards of a passive income, and whether you continue to work or not is irrelevant for the purposes of investing in real estate.

Your primary goal in investing should be to create a passive income. Passive income (or cash flow) is an income that is generated while you do virtually nothing for it. What it is not is a forty-hour week at work earning $25 per hour. In real estate, it is holding an asset that is not only paying for itself, but it is also paying you.

That is important, so take the time to think about it for a moment . . . You *want* the property that you invest in to pay for itself by way of rental returns—sounds good, doesn't it? But if you buy the right property, not only will it pay for itself (it covers the mortgage repayments and the other costs related to owning a rental property), but it will also pay you money after all its expenses. It's true; there are properties out there that will put money into your bank account instead of taking it out. You just need to find them.

Another factor to consider is, do you think lenders will be prepared to continue financing your portfolio when your current properties (and possibly your future properties) are *costing* you money? These 'assets' are putting nothing into your pocket despite the efforts of some telling you that they are. Don't get me wrong. They probably will give you a passive rental income some day; it just won't be today. You might be looking at up to a decade before that income is realised. And right now, the bank will see them as your liabilities, because they *cost* you money to own; they are not a passive income, and right now, they are not even paying for themselves.

Do these positively geared properties sound too good to be true? Do you believe that finding a property at a bargain basement price, which will cover your mortgage repayments as well as give you some change, is next to impossible? Well, I am here to say that they *are* out there. The one thing you need to remember (particularly if you are losing hope of finding that property) is that there is a *continual* stream of undervalued properties becoming available on the market; you just need to keep looking.

> *The key goal for you here is to be actively seeking positively geared properties at all times, not just when you think that you are ready to make the purchase. Take the opportunity to develop your research skills, and you may be surprised to find that when you discover a really good deal that you absolutely* cannot *pass up, you will think outside the box in order to make it happen.*

Sometimes it's a divorce settlement, a deceased estate, mortgage repossession, or even unpaid council rates that can land this little gem in your lap, so keep your eyes and ears open at *all* times.

Chapter 2

DO! SHORT-TERM CAPITAL GROWTH

Short-term capital growth—it's quite the mouthful, isn't it? I stopped to wonder whether I should define the words 'short-term' and decided that I should, because to me, it is not instant nor is it overnight (as we would all like to hope), and I want to explain why. I define short-term as between six and eighteen months; you may define it differently, but you also may hope to win the lottery tomorrow night. In my mind, though, even if you do win the lottery tomorrow night, I would still think that it takes more than a couple of weeks to cash that cheque, and even longer to actually win the lottery.

So nothing appears to be *instant* to me; everything takes time—baking a cake takes time, doing the grocery shopping takes time, educating yourself takes time . . . Well, you get the point, *everything* takes time, so of course, investing in real estate to create capital growth takes time.

'Capital growth', for the purposes of real estate, is essentially where the value of the property is increased. So when I use the term 'short-term capital growth', I am referring to an increase in the value of your property which occurs within the next eighteen months.

It is important to you because it will give you more leverage in the real estate market much sooner than waiting to see the gradual five—or ten-year-profit from your portfolio. It will allow you to purchase more positively geared properties more regularly and thereby secure the growth of your portfolio, your assets, and your income.

Remember *equity*? Well, capital growth creates more equity in your property. Real estate investors should always be seeking more equity in their properties as efficiently and effectively as they can so that they can continue growing their portfolio successfully.

Let's look at ways for you to gain short-term capital growth with your next property investment in the real estate market:-

1) Build Your Property

Immediate wealth is created from the moment that the property is complete. Yes, it can be a tedious journey, but the reward is significant capital growth that can be realised in the short-term. The building process averages about six months from start to finish for a standard residential home, and you can literally make a profit of anywhere between $40,000 and $100,000 for just taking the time to build. This kind of short-term profit is very rarely seen with the purchase of a pre-existing house.

The capital growth advantage aside, tenants love new properties. So the tenant vacancy rates should be quite low, and you can potentially receive a higher rental return than the surrounding older style properties, creating a positively geared property. The repairs and maintenance will also be minimal over the first few years of the home's life.

In Australia, the Tax Office also allows depreciation (or wear and tear) to be claimed in relation to fixtures and fittings in properties for some years, whereas a pre-existing home has already depreciated over the years for the purposes of tax. With a newly built home, you will be claiming depreciation at a time when those items are the most valuable thereby giving you a higher return.

Similarly, you can claim a capital works deduction for the construction expenses such as payments to tradespeople, architect and engineering fees, as well as the cost of building a retaining wall or swimming pool. The deductions that you can apply at the end of the financial year is currently set at 2.5 per cent of the costs per year for up to forty years.

There are definitely plenty of reasons to build your next investment property rather than buy a pre-existing home, but the immediate increase in the value of your portfolio (your equity) is, by far, my favourite excuse to build.

Short-term capital growth? Check. Positively geared property? Check. Great tax benefits? Check. Next property, here I come!

2) Renovate and/or Extend

Now, I know that this isn't everyone's cup of tea, but if you're anything like me and get excited by the idea of renovating and decorating, do it! Use your talent. You might be able to see a property that is in such a state of disrepair, and the possibilities just run rampant through your mind. While other people will steer well away from it, to you, it's a challenge, an opportunity, and the potential seems limitless in your mind. Well, then grab that deal and enjoy your passion to not only make it feel fresh and beautiful, but also to increase its value.

A large number of older-style properties are a basic design, so from the perspective of extending, they can easily become a modern home with extra bedrooms and an en suite. For example, the small bedroom (that was originally the front verandah, which someone along the line decided to enclose to add an extra room to the property) is generally placed next to the master bedroom, so a doorway can be placed in that adjoining wall and it will make the perfect size ensuite.

Similarly, a lot of old designs will have a lounge and dining area that are on the adjacent side of the house, so a hallway and additional bedrooms can be added to the home after extending the roofline and adding floor space.

It is simply a matter of imagination and creativity to be able to turn an old two-bedroom weatherboard house into a four-bedroom-plus-study and two-bathroom home, and this is simply because most old homes are a basic square or rectangular design and don't have the hurdle of a solid brick structure to negotiate and overcome.

As a (*very*) general rule, you can expect your renovation costs to triple in value, if it is of a high standard. So, say you spend $20,000 on a renovation project; you *should* be able to see a minimum increase in the property's value by $60,000. Of course, this varies from house to house and location to location, and depends on the amount of work that you are savvy enough to do yourself, the quality of the workmanship, and any unexpected expenses that may arise (such as discovering that you need to rewire the entire home!) So this is only a rough guide for your consideration.

Renovating or extending can bring short-term capital growth to you by either selling the property at a higher price than you paid for it and moving on to your next investment, or simply increasing your rental return and the equity in your portfolio. Whichever way you decide to go, it is a worthwhile avenue to help you achieve your goals.

It may take six months to complete the project, but it also may only take a week; it may cost a significant amount of money, or it may cost a little. The capital works deduction will also be available to you when you renovate or extend, so keep this in mind when considering how much you plan to spend on your investment.

Find the ugly duckling, and turn it into a beautiful home that future buyers or potential tenants can see themselves living in and enjoying. Keep in mind though, during the renovation, who your prospective target is. Is it a family? Or is it an executive couple? Your design ideas need to be based on the requirements of that particular demographic in order to achieve the maximum potential for that particular property. So don't get carried away with ideas of what you, personally, would like, because that can tend to see you blow your budget and waste valuable time.

Whether you choose to sell or you choose to hold on to the property, make certain that you have researched both the costs and the time that it will take you. Remember, your time and your money are extremely precious to you in growing your portfolio of properties. So don't waste either of them shopping for tapware that you have always dreamt of or in buying top-of-the-range door handles to go into your investment property, if it doesn't suit your targeted demographic.

With building, renovating, or extending, you do need time and you will need funds, but it can create a short-term capital growth that is not provided by just buying an established, ready-to-go property.

3) Sub-divide

In the most basic terms, 'subdivision' is the cutting up of an existing block of land to make two or more blocks of land. Other types of subdivision include

a) **Strata-titling**—this is the vertical subdivision of property, such as units and apartments;

b) **Community titling**—this is the horizontal subdivision of property, such as villas and townhouses; and

c) **Company titling**—this is the subdivision of a company building that is sold as shares (however, the sale of shares and the financing can be quite difficult, so at this stage I urge you to steer clear of this form of subdivision).

For the purposes of this book, I would just like to focus on the most common form of subdivision, being the splitting of a residential block regardless of whether or not there is a pre-existing building on the land.

If you are looking for property, always try to find blocks that are in a position to be subdivided, either now or in the near future. Often you can gauge this yourself by looking at the neighbouring properties. For example, if there are two mail boxes on what appears to be one property, one numbered 22a and the other 22b, the zoning for a subdivision is probably already there, and you just need confirmation with the local council; they are the ones that hold the guidelines of who, what, when, where, and why subdivisions are permitted in their local area.

New developments in the area may show you that a standard-sized block is approximately 700 square metres, and you may find an older property nearby that is actually 2,300 square metres; it can indicate to you that there may be potential to subdivide the parcel of land into three separate blocks. Now, I am not encouraging you to just go off your own opinion; you are best to speak with the relevant person in the local council offices and then put yourself in a 'worst-case scenario' frame of mind, but you will find indicators if you take the time to look.

Let's say that in the case of a 2,300-square-metre-block, the council has said to you that it could potentially be approved for a subdivision into three blocks prior to you signing the contract. You should assume that you can divide the property into two parcels of land; however, you may discover that once you own the property and it comes time to prepare and lodge your application for the subdivision, you can, in fact, divide the property into four blocks. Bonus! Three more properties to be added to your portfolio!

Remember though, it works both ways; something unforeseen may also prevent or delay your planned subdivision, so be prepared. Even some of the best-laid plans can go off track at times, and in this case, you just need to stay positive and keep moving forwards.

Importantly, don't allow yourself to be fooled by the local real estate agents promoting and advertising that the land *can* be subdivided and offering the property at an above-market price; after all, the subdivision hasn't happened yet. Often they haven't even confirmed this with the local council and are merely making the assumption based on the surrounding developments (as you just did) or, worse, relying on the word of the seller. So be very wary when you take an agent's word at face value; you may find yourself stuck with a property for which you paid too much, which has no hopes of a subdivision, and which has very little use to you, as an investor. Thus, it is essential that you, yourself, speak with the local governing body to know what you are getting yourself into.

~

Capital growth on real estate does inevitably occur over time, but the short-term capital growth created by building, renovating, extending, or subdividing a property will enable you to reach your goals a lot faster than simply waiting for the real estate market to steadily increase over time.

> *Target* short-term capital growth *on all your real estate investments; it will give the opportunity to sell the property for a profit, increase your rental returns, or boost the equity that you have in your portfolio.*

Your task? Add 'short-term capital growth potential' to your criteria while you are actively searching for that next positively geared property.

Remember also, once you have created that capital growth, you would also like to see a positively geared property sitting in your portfolio; capital growth is one thing to consider, but it's also important that you do your calculations to make certain that you are not setting yourself up for a negatively geared 'asset'.

Chapter 3

DON'T! BE AFRAID OF RISK

What can I say about risk and the all-encompassing fear of failure? I would like to say this—I have heard all the excuses about why you 'can't do it', and they are just that . . . *excuses*. The reality is that fear makes us, by our very nature, find the reasons why we cannot do it; if you are really serious about taking control of your future in property investing, then you will need to eliminate 'I *can't* do it' from your mind and replace it with 'How *can* I do it?'

The use of words and the effect that they can have on us and our actions (or reactions) has been long discussed in a wide variety of researched topics over time. Even studies offering advice on an everyday task, such as parenting, highlight the importance of the use of words and how they can affect the human mind from a very young age. For example, in order to deal with something as simple as a child running in the house, it is suggested that using the term 'please walk' is far more successful in stopping the child from running than using the words 'don't run'.

Simply removing the negative word can have a positive and powerful outcome on our way of thinking. Try to eliminate the word 'can't' from your vocabulary when it comes to the goals for yourself and for your investment portfolio; after all, 'Where there is a will, there is a way,' and your job is to find it.

Now, if you just *won't* set high goals to aim for because you are scared of failure, just admit that that is the cause. If risk scares you, then make a choice to continually remind yourself that no self-made millionaire became successful without taking a risk, without that first leap of faith.

> *Risk is an* essential *element of success.*

How do you view risk? Does a $1 million block of units sound riskier than a $350,000 house?

It really depends on the two properties and on the research that you have undertaken. For instance, the idea of purchasing a block of six units for a cost of $1 million can seem far more daunting than purchasing a single residential home for $350,000, but take the time to break it down and see that despite it *sounding* scary, it can, in actual fact, prove to be quite profitable in comparison, as well as help you minimise the risk.

Here's why: Because instead of that one property, at a cost of $350,000, you were looking to add to your portfolio, you are now looking at purchasing six rental properties that can be tenanted, and they only cost you $166,666 each. Bargain, right? Well, it gets better . . .

Understand that a block of units will generally be sold under one title (meaning that the residences haven't been legally separated into individual properties yet), and if you subdivide those units by strata-titling, you will not only be creating short-term capital growth and increasing the property's value, but will also be expanding your portfolio by adding five extra properties to it. Sounds good, doesn't it? Want more?

Here is your income . . . With the block of units you now have six incomes; not just one, as you would with a single dwelling, but six. Let's say that you can achieve $270 per week in rental returns for each apartment, which is $ $1,620 per week. Sounds okay, doesn't it?

Well, if you held an interest-only mortgage in the full amount of $1 million at 5.9 per cent, your weekly repayments would be approximately $1,131 per week, leaving you a passive income of $489 per week!

Mortgage Repayments ($1,000,000 @ 5.9%) = $1,131
Rental Return ($270 × 6) = $1,620

Profit = *$489*

Again, that calculation doesn't take into account the real estate management fees, council rates, times that a unit may be vacant, or even the occasional repairs. But as I said earlier, these extra costs are generally covered by the tax benefits available to you for owning the property. This is merely a guide into training your mind for success in the real estate market, reduce your fear of risk, and offer you the points to consider when evaluating whether a particular property ticks all the boxes in order for you to want to add it to your portfolio.

So with the block of six units, you have achieved

1. Capital growth by subdividing,
2. Positive cash flow, and
3. Reduced risk by spreading the risk over six residential properties.

Now, if you decide that all *still* sounds a little too scary, then your alternative is to buy the other property at $350,000.

Let's say that you have a mortgaged amount of $350,000 under the same terms as I mentioned above; then you will *need* your weekly rental return to be at least $396 per week *just* to cover the current mortgage repayments . . . no additional costs, just the mortgage alone. And that, to me, sounds far riskier than the idea of buying the $1 million property.

> *Take risks . . .*
>
> *If you win, you will be happy.*
>
> *If you lose, you will be wise.*
>
> Author Unknown

Risk is also reduced if you are prepared to ride any waves of decline or rise in the property market without 'freaking out' and selling your property because fear (or greed) took a hold of you. It is generally recommended that property investors hold on to their property for a minimum term of between five and ten years, because historically, despite the waves, property does go up in value over the long term. You should ideally be looking at holding on to your property for this recommended period because the entry costs, such as stamp duty and legal fees, are quite high, so you will need time to recover from them in addition to achieving the long-term capital growth from your property.

Essentially, I want you to get excited about the potential of what may sound risky and recognise that the vast majority of 'risk' can be eliminated if you are prepared to hold on to your property for the long term and you take the time to do your sums and your homework—make it a calculated risk, which leads me to my next chapter, *Do the Research!*

Chapter 4

DO! THE RESEARCH

I should start this chapter by saying that getting advice from the local real estate agent is *not* what I mean by 'do the research'. Sure, they can have some handy information like the expansion of the local shopping centre and the development of a major road, but they are there to make money too; their income relies on making a sale, and we've all heard the creative estate agent descriptions—'cosy', 'renovators dream', 'low-maintenance', and so on and so forth, not to mention the manipulated photographs of properties in order to create the illusion of space. Real estate agents need to sell properties to make their commissions—that is their job. *Your* job is to do your *own* research on the property and on the suburb in which you are looking to buy.

So I'm guessing that many of you immediately will think to yourselves, 'Yeah, yeah, yeah, check local rental returns, compare property prices in the area, blah, blah, blah.' It's true; that is all very important information for you to have researched. However, if you are interested in real estate investment, then I would think that you have probably already looked at that stuff. So what I would like to discuss instead is the research that is, more often than not, overlooked by the average investor.

The Internet is aptly known as the super highway of information, so there is no excuse not to do your own research. I know that I could not live without the Internet and the wealth of knowledge that it holds. With the click of a button, you can discover everything from the population of an area to the exact distance of the nearest train station.

So some things to consider that will assist you in the medium-to-long-term capital growth of your property and also ensure minimal vacancy rates of your investment include

1) **Population growth.** You need to research not only the suburb that you are looking to buy in, but also the surrounding suburbs. It is especially important to note if there has been a significant decline in population recently. If there has been, the recovery period for that particular suburb may take quite some time, resulting in a property that may not be feasible to invest in as the population may continue to decrease and, consequently, it may reduce the value of both the property and also the rental returns available to you.

2) **Nearest schools.** Families need schools and the convenience of one being located nearby can be a great marketing tool for either prospective tenants or future purchasers. It is also important that the schools are reputable, so try to establish that information, not only through Internet research but also local opinion.

3) **Recent and planned developments in the area.** This can show you what the general forecast for the area's growth is; if a major grocery store is not even slightly interested in moving to the area, or the local council is knocking back several proposed developments at this stage, the capital growth of your property is likely to be further into the future than you had hoped for.

4) **Distance to the nearest public transport and airport.** A suburb and its economy's growth generally centralises around a convenient transport infrastructure, so this is something to be aware of when you are looking to invest. Take the time to research the distances with an online maps web site; you simply enter directions from the address of the property that you are looking at to the relevant point of interest—whether it's a bus stop, train station or airport—and it will calculate the exact distance as well as the time that it takes to get there, whether it's by walking or driving.

5) **Scarcity of land.** If finding land in a particular area is difficult, and some has just hit the market, grab it! You can generally be certain that the suburb is well established and will probably not suffer any sudden or rapid declines in the population or the local economy,

which will give you confidence in the potential capital growth of the property and in the area that you are looking to invest in.

6) **Crime rates.** As a tenant, would you like to live in the street that has the worst reputation when it comes to crime? Probably not. So ensure that your property is in a more desirable location for your tenants; the last thing you need is for your investment to sit there vacant for any significant amount of time, waiting for someone to move in due to a poor reputation regarding crime. You can find general information about a suburb's crime rate with your Internet search engine.

Now all you need to do is just make the Internet, and sites such as *myRPdata*, the *Bureau of Statistics*, and *Whereis* (or your international equivalents) your best friends. These web sites are your eyes and ears; use them often and use them well.

> *This is your* business—*treat it like one.*

You wouldn't go all gung-ho into a business (I hope); you would have a thorough criteria and would set a structure in place in order to obtain your ultimate goals. Do the same with each and every property that you are considering investing in because even if it meets the most basic of your criteria of being positively geared, if there has been a sudden decline in population recently, the capital growth may be off somewhere in the distant future, and you will just have to keep your fingers crossed, hoping that the market and your rental return doesn't decrease in that time also—ultimately turning your 'ideal' investment property into a complete lemon, which, let's face it, you don't want sitting in your portfolio, chewing up your cash.

So do the research (often referred to as 'due diligence'); you can get a free suburb profile from *myRPdata*, you can obtain free maps and distances to points of interest from *Whereis*, and you can get free suburb and population data from the *Australian Bureau of Statistics*. Take the time to use these and similar web sites; it's a lot safer than just rolling the dice and hoping you come up trumps, or relying on the local real estate agent's sales pitch, only to discover that the local primary school is about to close down.

Your research is your security, your own personal insurance protecting you from purchasing the wrong property. So use the web sites and invest time in your research on each and every property that you are looking at adding to your portfolio.

After all your research, an added bonus is that you might discover an absolute gem of a town; well, good news—you already have all the information in your hot little hand for your next investment property. I wouldn't recommend you buying up the whole town though, so if you do find a great location to invest in, I encourage you to be cautious and remember

> *Spreading properties in different local areas*
>
> *= minimising the risk*

Chapter 5

DO! REMEMBER 'CAVEAT EMPTOR'

I have outlined what makes your purchase a good deal, which will, hopefully, make your property search a little easier. I have also explained to you that you need to do the research to make certain that you are buying the right real estate for your portfolio and ensuring its capital growth, but now I want to explain to you the importance and the concept of 'caveat emptor'.

'Caveat emptor' is a Latin term that means 'let the buyer beware'. It is derived from *caveat*, meaning 'may he beware' and *emptor*, meaning 'buyer'. It is essentially the principle that the buyer alone is responsible for ensuring the quality and suitability of goods before a purchase is made.

Why is it so important for the buyer to beware? It's simply because a contract is a legally binding document. When you sign on the dotted line, you are bound by law to follow through with the purchase. The only way that you can be released from your obligation to purchase the property is if one or more of the conditions are not met and not if you just change your mind because you found a better deal down the road (and let's hope that doesn't happen).

The contract in relation to the sale of real estate is pretty standard and outlines the legal obligations and duties of all parties; however, more often than not, there are additional clauses that will be added prior to all parties signing and will commonly include

1) 'Subject to finance approval'

This is a common clause which you will need to add to the contract if you will be borrowing money to buy the property.

The important thing for you to note about this particular clause is that you really do need to state which lending institution you will be applying to for finance. The reason for this is that if the bank that you had in mind for your purchase says no, then the people selling the property can ask you to continue to apply to other lenders. Sometimes there will be another lender that will be prepared to offer you a mortgage on the property; however, the terms may not be very favourable to you. For instance, they may offer you the loan, but at a much higher interest rate than you were ever prepared to pay (because you want a positively geared property). So it is imperative to state in the finance clause of your contract which lending institution you will be applying to for purchasing the property or, at the very least, state the words 'purchaser's choice' as your financier.

You are not bound to stick with that lender if you find a better deal at another institution; the seller will just be happy that your finance has been approved. Adding the actual financier or 'purchaser's choice' to this clause simply prevents you from being stuck with a bad loan that has unreasonable repayments if the vendor forces your hand on the purchase.

2) 'Subject to satisfactory building and pest inspection'

You, yourself, should not only visually inspect the property that you are buying, but should also obtain a building and pest inspection from a qualified and independent professional. The purpose of the inspection is to identify any major defects or safety hazards associated with the property. It won't include an estimate of the costs to rectify any defects, but it will give you an idea of the headache you could potentially be dealing with in the future while comparing it to buildings of approximately the same age that have been similarly constructed and reasonably maintained.

Understandably, this clause will not apply to the purchase of land only; it is primarily for the purposes of a pre-existing building that you intend to rent or sell in the near future. If you plan to knock the building down, I would suggest that the condition of the property is of no major concern to you, so it's not really necessary to waste the time or the money in undertaking a building and pest inspection unless you believe that it will provide you with the ability to negotiate a price reduction.

Let's look at the type of defects that will be examined by the building inspector.

- **Damage**—this is where the building material or item has deteriorated or is not fit for its purpose.

- **Distortion, warping, and twisting**—sometimes an item has moved out of shape or moved from its position, and repair or replacement may need to be done.

- **Water penetration and dampness**—where moisture has gained access to any unplanned or unacceptable areas. It can also offer you some insight into whether it has been a flood-affected property in the past and the extent of the damage that may happen if another flood should occur in the future.

- **Material deterioration**—if an item has defects such as rusting, rotting, corrosion, or decay. Remember again that this will be compared to other homes of a similar age and similar construction, so some deterioration may be relatively normal given the age of the property.

- **Operational**—when an item does not work the way that it was intended to.

- **Installation (including omissions)**—sometimes the way that an item has been installed is unacceptable, is not working, or is simply absent.

The pest side of the inspection is relatively easy to understand. Termites (or white ants) are the major concern here. Sometimes termites will be found in surrounding wooden fences, but provided that there is no presence within the walls or ceilings of the property, this is very treatable and at a low cost. However, if termites have been found within the building, you should know that this can cause significant cost to you in structural replacement and repairs.

If any defects are found, it can help you negotiate a cheaper price on the property. The only time you will find that there is very little protection under this clause is in a mortgagee sale (where the bank has repossessed the property from the previous owner), as the property will often be sold 'as is, where is'. Therefore, regardless of an inspection, you will still be required to purchase the property, so you need to be mindful of this if you are entering into a contract with a mortgagee in possession. You still may be permitted to conduct a building and pest inspection, but it will have very little effect on your legal obligation to purchase the property. So if those dreaded termites are found, I'm afraid that you will be stuck with the little critters, so tread very carefully here. It may be an idea to request these inspections prior to signing the contract; however, it will be at the discretion of the seller as to whether they will allow it or not.

A combined pre-purchase inspection, including both the building and pest, can vary in price, which currently starts from $350, depending on the size of the property. However, the long-term stress of a dud property sitting in your portfolio, which becomes more and more costly due to significant and unexpected deterioration, can prove to be much more expensive in both time and money, and, let's face it, both of these things can be better spent looking for your next property.

3) 'Subject to satisfactory due diligence'

A further clause that you, as an investor, will want to request adding is 'subject to the purchaser's satisfactory due diligence' or something similar. I say 'something similar' because it is largely dependent on your plans for the property. If you plan to subdivide immediately, and based on your preliminary research it will be approved, you might add a clause relating to the local council's approval of that subdivision, but generally, the term 'due diligence' will cover a range of these things.

A due diligence clause is essentially your option to undertake further research to ensure that the property is suitable for the use that you intend. The vendor may not approve of this clause, but it is definitely worthwhile for you to ask. It will give you the opportunity to have the contract in place as well as allow you the time to do the additional research to make sure that the property meets the criteria of being a good investment to add to your portfolio.

It will allow you time to speak with the local council if you are considering building, renovating, extending, or subdividing; it will give you time to make certain that it will be a positively geared property; and it will give you time to research the suburb statistics for future economic growth and rental occupancy rates.

> *Be aware of the fact that the contract is* legally binding *on you; therefore, you need to make sure that you structure the additional clauses properly for your protection and that you have a building and pest inspection conducted by a qualified and independent professional.*

You want this property to be an asset to you, and failing to do these simple things can potentially turn the property deal of a lifetime into a liability that you will wish you had never laid your eyes on.

Chapter 6

DON'T! UNDER-INSURE

Okay, you've got your new investment property. What next? You need to protect it, and you need to protect you. You need insurance. Asset protection is the key to holding on to your portfolio; after all, you've done all the hard work in acquiring your properties, the last thing that you want is to lose them because they weren't protected properly. So let's run through the types of insurance that you will need to look at.

1) Property Insurance

This is the first and most predominant form of insurance for your real estate investment. However, what you need to understand, as an investor, is that many people will actually under-insure their property to save a couple of dollars or to save time in actually figuring out what the replacement cost is. *Do not* under-insure your property!

A lot of people don't realise that if property is worth $200,000 and it is insured for only $100,000, the insurer can (and more than likely will) only pay out a total sum of $50,000 'because you were only insured for half of what it was worth'. Figure that one out! But it makes perfect sense to the insurance company, and you will have no recourse for the $150,000 that you are now out of pocket, because it was all right there in front of your eyes in the fine print. So be very wary of your insurance policy, and know the value of your assets.

Protect your assets; they are your income streams and financial growth. Look after them, as they do you. Don't simply find the most cost-effective insurance policy and think that it ends there because it can cost you very dearly in the long run if you discover that certain events were not underwritten in the policy document or if you have under-insured.

~

Non-disclosure (not telling the insurance company all the relevant information or failing to answer their questions honestly) can prevent the policy from being paid out at all, and under-valuing your assets can prevent you being paid out the full insured amount. A variety of circumstances and situations can affect your right to claim under an insurance policy, and with the reputations held by these particular companies, it is difficult to say that an insurance provider will not do anything and everything that they can to avoid honouring the policy that you hold with them. Worse news is that it will be legal, so your research and a thorough understanding of the insurance policy and its terms and conditions is the key to avoid having any of your assets fall prey to one of the many loopholes in the insurance world.

I once heard, and I couldn't agree more, that the most common lie that is told is 'I have read and agree to the terms and conditions.' Even if you tried to convince me that you are one of the minority that *do* read the terms and conditions in every contract that you are entering into, I wouldn't buy it. I'm not even sure that those who indulge in a lottery are aware that it is a contract and that there are terms and conditions attached to the ticket that you just bought. How about the song that you just downloaded or the web site that you just joined? You got it . . . terms and conditions that you *agreed* to, but you didn't *really* read them, did you?

When it comes to insuring such a significant asset as your portfolio and each individual property involved, you *need* to read the terms and conditions that are in the policy document. As boring as it is, if you find out after a flood that you weren't covered by 'acts of God', you will wish that you *had* bored yourself to tears with the fine print because you will soon discover that you are relying on your other income sources or getting another loan to cover the loss and the damage caused to that one property.

2) Landlord Insurance

As an investor tenanting out your property, this insurance is a must. As much faith as we would all like to have in our tenants, there are bad ones out there, so whatever you do, make sure that you hold a landlord insurance policy. Regardless of whether your property is self-managed, managed by a real estate, or only rented out for short periods.

Landlord insurance can cover loss of rent, whether it was

- defaulted by tenants that abandoned the property;
- a court-ordered eviction;
- malicious damage that leaves your property untenantable;
- death or hardship of the tenant;
- or the tenant refusing you access while rent remains unpaid.

Additionally, where you can make a claim for rent, you can also be covered for re-letting fees, the cost of changing the locks, the removal of rubbish or goods, and even legal representation fees.

This insurance covers you not only for loss of rent and the costs associated with it but also for any deliberate and malicious damage done to your property by your tenants or their guests.

Unfortunately, despite yours and/or your agent's thorough background and reference checks on the tenancy applicants, you may still end up landing the 'tenants from hell': the ones that refuse to leave the property, those that put holes in the walls, or ones that steal your furnishings.

On top of all these inclusions, you will also be covered for any accidental injury that may be caused to your tenant on the property up to an amount of $20 million, but remember that lack of any appropriate safety measures in a rental property can also prevent you from being paid out. Know your policy!

Landlord insurance for residential properties starts from only $280 per year, which is a very small price to pay for the peace of mind that it will give you as an investor.

~

Property and landlord insurance aside, what happens if the worst should occur, and you are made redundant, or have an accident, or any number of other unfortunate events that can prevent you from working and cause you financial hardship? You will learn very quickly how many people would like your attention if you miss a couple of payments. Which brings me to the other forms of insurance that you need to look at as an investor.

3) Income Protection Insurance

Income protection insurance will be your lifeline if you should suddenly be made redundant, become seriously ill, or injured and cannot continue working.

Your investment business needs you, absolutely, but if by some misfortune you find yourself unable to work during the course of *building up* your property portfolio, then you can bet your bottom dollar that you are also going to find yourself in need of an income, and fast.

The good news is that with income protection insurance, insurance companies can pay you up to 85 per cent of your current income for up to two years, with some even offering up to five years, if you happen to find yourself out of action for any number of reasons.

With the steady and successful growth of your positively geared properties, even if you do find yourself unable to work, you will have an income stream from your investments that you do not need to physically work for and which will, at the very least, pay for themselves. If you are at a point in your investing where you still need your employment, income protection insurance is a necessity.

4) Life Insurance

Most people understand the concept of life insurance; it is basically an agreed sum of money that is paid out in the event of your death.

You should hold a life insurance policy for an amount that can pay out all your loans and outstanding debts, so if you owe $1 million in funds to banks or lenders, insure yourself for a minimum of $1 million.

Of course that means, with your growing portfolio, you are going to need to reassess your policy on a regular basis. That can be a little annoying, sure, but the fact is that it can save your family from even more heartache of having to maintain your debts for you once you pass away, so it makes the time spent reviewing your policies worthwhile in the long run.

As with all your insurances, know your policy; know how much it will pay out, under what circumstances it will pay out, and when it will pay out. It is no good to you finding out that you weren't allowed to go swimming with sharks, or hiking Mount Everest, after your demise.

You should also update your last will and testament as your portfolio grows. It is recommended that you take the time to specify in this document that the insurance funds released from any life policy are specifically to pay off any outstanding debts first and foremost, and then the rest of the estate can be dealt with and managed more efficiently. What nicer gift to leave your partner, your children, or your grandchildren than a passive income generated from your property portfolio?

~

You still can't be bothered reading all that fine print? Sounds like too much hard work? Then all I can say is find a good insurance broker and let them know exactly what you need to be covered.

It is wise for you to educate yourself on insurance as a form of asset protection. Insurance is extremely important to you; you need it! It is also extremely important to your properties; they need it! Understand it, and it may just be your saving grace. Make an error in selecting your coverage or overlook the fine print, and it could turn out to be your worst nightmare.

Chapter 7

DO! CREATE A COMPANY

This is a subject that could be a whole book on its own, so the information that I have provided is by no means thorough. Laws, rules, and regulations will vary from state to state and country to country. I urge you to be mindful of this as I, very briefly, run through why you should create a company (or companies) for your assets.

It is important to note that when I refer to the benefits of owning your assets under a company or a trust, I am *not* exclusively referring to positively geared property; the benefits are available to you, as a real estate investor, regardless of whether you are positively gearing or negatively gearing your properties.

Creating a company to hold your investment properties is another form of asset protection, and it also has some significant taxation benefits that you, as a 'natural' person, cannot access. Trusts can also have a similar effect, and it will be best for you to discuss which options suit you with your accountant or financial advisor.

There are a few predominant reasons that you are better off investing in property as a company rather than as an individual, and they are as follows:

1) **Asset protection.** As an individual, you have unlimited liability, so if something goes wrong, then your personal possessions, as well as your business assets are at risk; whereas, with a company, your personal liability is limited to the amount that you have personally invested in the company.

2) **Income tax.** If you are hoping to achieve a substantial personal income from your investments, your personal income tax rate can reach up to 46.5 per cent, whereas the company tax rate is currently capped at 30 per cent.

3) **Taxable deductions.** As an individual, you also won't receive many of the taxable deductions that are available to the company structure.

4) **Tax planning.** As a company, you have more ability for tax planning by dividing the incomes among family members (e.g. your husband or wife) in order to reduce your income tax liability. As an individual, it is solely your income which may push you well over the 30 per cent capped tax rate that is available to companies.

Essentially, a company is its own separate entity. It stands alone for the purposes of legislation and taxation. It is its own person, it has its own identity, and it pays you as a shareholder by way of dividends, or as an employee by way of wage or salary, or even both. Trusts, however, are not their own entity like an individual or a company; they are a legally binding *relationship* between the trustee/s and the beneficiary/ies.

As an investor, you may consider holding your investments in a trust. There are a variety of trust structures available, including the Discretionary Family Trust, the Unit Trust, and the Hybrid Trust. Essentially when it comes to trusts, there is no 'one size fits all', and you will need to consult with your accountant, tax specialist, or lawyer when making your decision about which type of trust is suitable for you.

The trustee can be a natural person or a company that holds, manages, and sets aside the assets that are held in trust (such as real estate) until they are distributed to the beneficiary. The beneficiary is an individual or a company that is entitled to receive the assets that are held in trust and any profits made from those assets.

> ***Trustee*** = *holds and manages the assets.*
>
> ***Beneficiary*** = *receives the assets.*

The same person or company can also be both the trustee and the beneficiary.

A little confusing, isn't it? Companies, trusts, and the laws and taxes relevant to these business structures are really quite complex, and the benefits of a company and each different type of trust vary. You don't need to become an expert in the field, but it is important that you discuss both the advantages and the disadvantages of each business structure with a qualified professional to enable you to understand and decide which one is most suitable for your personal circumstances and your particular goals. Advantages include

> **Taxation.** Companies and trusts have a great range of tax benefits and deductions that are available to them, ones that are not available to people investing under their own name. Remembering that a trust is not acknowledged as its own separate entity, as a company is, the maximum taxable rate for personal income may still apply under a trust set-up, so you do need to speak with your accountant or financial advisor to establish your preferred business structure.
>
> The tax advantages of operating your real estate business under a company or trust are far too extensive to list here, and as I said earlier, the benefits will be specific to you and your locality, so spend the time researching and discussing them with a qualified professional that specialises in this field to ensure that you are maximising your portfolio's potential.
>
> **Getting sued.** Let's face it, we now live in a society where getting sued is not only possible, but if you are wealthy, it is highly probable.
>
> We've all heard the horror stories of people taking legal action against individuals and companies, sometimes for the most trivial of matters in order to gain a few dollars. As an individual (rather than a company), you will personally be the target, and your liability is *unlimited*, which means that you could lose absolutely everything that you have worked for, and you may find yourself handing over the keys not only to your investment properties but also to the family home and the car.
>
> However, because a company is an entity in its own right, it will be the only one affected by the legal action. It will still probably be quite traumatic for you, but generally it will have no direct effect on your *personal* assets. That is why I suggest that you need to create not only one, but multiple companies, as well as diversify the ownership with the properties that you hold (spread the risk) as your portfolio grows. This will ensure that if you ever do find yourself in the unfortunate situation of being sued, the damage can be limited by containing the fire within

the one company (that is holding only a few assets) being subjected to the flame, rather than a singular company that owns *all* the assets. You will still feel the burn, but you won't see absolutely everything that you have worked for turn to ashes.

The more properties you acquire over time, the more you will start to consider establishing new companies or trusts to hold a portion of those assets.

How many properties you hold under each company or trust and the value of real estate owned by each, is something that, again, you will need to discuss with your accountant or financial planner; there are simply too many variables and personal considerations for me to be able to give you the 'correct' business structuring and the magic numbers that apply to your circumstances. You might hold a number of companies as well as various trusts by the time you reach your goal, so consult regularly with a professional advisor as your portfolio grows.

~

I have offered here just a couple of reasons why you should establish a company or trust fund structure in your business, and I remind you that this guide is designed to outline the dos and don'ts for investing in real estate.

Creating a company or establishing a trust is an extremely important part of real estate investing, so discuss all the available options in detail with your accountant regarding the avenues and business structures that are best suited to you for your investment strategies.

Remember, when considering your business structure that

> *a company is* a stand-alone entity with one or more directors managing it; and
>
> a *trust* is a legally recognised relationship between the trustee and the beneficiary.

As an investor in real estate, creating a company or a trust is a necessity, much like insurance, in ensuring your asset protection. So set up your business correctly at the outset in order to save yourself any undue hardship in the future.

Chapter 8

DON'T! AVOID YOUR TAXES

They're there; what are you going to do? For better or worse, taxes exist, and as the saying goes, they are as certain as death. So deal with them. Isn't it better to have some money rather than none at all?

There are a number of people out there who start to acquire investment properties, and their initial reaction is to avoid taxes. That could be because of the principles that they were taught from a young age, or because obtaining professional advice was too expensive for them to consider, or any other number of reasons personal to them. Whatever the reason, taxes should *not* be avoided. It can cost you dearly financially if you get caught, and it can even land you in jail; it's not really worth it if you can't even enjoy your wealth, is it?

One particular situation which stands out in my mind was where an investment property was purchased and shortly after, the opportunity arose to subdivide. It was a large block and would not get in the way of the existing house, so it made perfect sense to subdivide and build rather than just build a second house on the one property.

It was decided to just build the additional house and reap the rewards of an extra rental income, leaving them with one block of land that had two separate dwellings on it. Firstly, this is never really an 'ideal' property for a real estate agent to sell, and secondly, it completely wastes the clear and immediate profit that could have been created, significantly boosting the equity and their asset pool. In this particular case, the assets would have increased by at least $200,000. They would have created a second block of land by subdividing, and they would have built, so they had two avenues of short-term capital growth as well as the ownership of a further property added to their portfolio.

Let's run through another scenario. Assume that you purchase a property with a house on it for $160,000, and the market value for vacant land in that particular area is averaging $80,000. If you subdivide, chopping the block in half, you have immediately created an additional property for your portfolio worth around $80,000. Then, by going ahead and building, you could create a further profit of between $50,000 and $100,000 (as I discussed in the chapter on short-term capital growth). Let's say, in this scenario, $80,000 has been achieved from the subdivision and $70,000 has been achieved at the completion of the building process.

Capital Growth Example:

Profit from subdividing = *$ 80,000*
Profit from building = *$ 70,000*

Total Profit (equity gained) = *$150,000*

You still have your initial property, but from that you have generated two forms of short-term capital growth amounting to $150,000, equity on your newly developed property, as well as two rental incomes from what was originally just one property.

Sounds good, right? You could have created even more had you decided to build a duplex or units on the second block. So do the research and discuss your options with the local council and an experienced builder on how to get the most profit that you can from your investment property.

If two houses are placed on the one block, it just doesn't increase the land value; it's still an $80,000 block, rather than two $80,000 blocks.

But I digress . . . The point of my story on this particular individuals purchase is that this new asset of a residential building was not going to be on its own piece of land; they were not going to subdivide. No way! No how! The reasoning behind this was 'because I don't want an additional rates bill each year'. Did I miss something here? Profit of $200,000 plus an additional property for your portfolio versus a $560 tax loss in council rates each year. I know which one I would have choosen.

Now, let me go back to my original point. Let's assume that in the worst-case scenario, the tax office helps themselves to 50 per cent of the $150,000 that you just made by subdividing and building. That would still leave you with $75,000 profit—leverage for your next property investment. Isn't that still better than nothing? Sure, you lost $75,000, but you also gained $75,000, which wasn't available to you before. Is avoiding taxes really not worth growing your assets and your property portfolio? This equation is not based on any particular circumstances or any particular tax; it is merely to demonstrate that 50 per cent of nothing, is, well, nothing, whereas 50 per cent of something will at least be something.

There are plenty of perfectly legal tax benefits available to real estate investors. All you really need to do is educate yourself in investing and in the tax incentives that are available to you as well as seek *professional* advice. Be very wary of backyard tax advice—you know the kind, the advice you can get from your brother-in-law that lives overseas, the mate down at the local tavern over a few beers, or the friend next door that 'knows everything about everything'. Simply because, the information that they give you can do more harm than good; what is relevant to them and their situation may not be at all relevant to you.

Many investors fail to obtain the full taxation benefits available to them, so it is necessary to have a knowledgeable tax accountant, preferably one who is a specialist in real estate investing, in addition to you to having some basic understanding. Some common tax-related mistakes made by many real estate investors that you should be aware of are as follows:

1) **Depreciation.** A tax deduction that is underestimated by so many property investors is depreciation (wear and tear). Tax depreciation is claimable on various items in your property that decline in value over time. It is also a deduction where you do not need to spend any money in order to claim it back, so it is well worth your while to organise a qualified quantity surveyor to complete a depreciation report in relation to each and every property that you add to your portfolio. A tax depreciation schedule can cost from $450 for each property, but you will find that the tax benefits you gain from it

will far outweigh the cost. The schedule that will be prepared for you is a forty-year forecast of the building itself, as well as all other depreciable items such as kitchen appliances, air-conditioning units, light fittings, floor coverings, curtains, furniture, and more, so once it's done, you won't need to do it again in a hurry.

2) **Timing.** Strategically timing your purchase for the end of the financial year can help absorb some of the major costs associated with your new investment because you can claim the deductions almost immediately. This is definitely an advantage, particularly if it's a newly built property where you can receive the full depreciation allowance.

3) **Getting the right loan.** For tax purposes it is recommended that your investment properties have an interest-only loan because there is no tax benefit on the principal amount (the actual amount borrowed), only on the interest portion of your loan. For example, if you have a $350,000 principal plus interest loan taken out over a period of twenty-five years at 6 per cent interest, your weekly repayments would be about $520 per week. Whereas under the same loan terms, an interest-only loan would cost you approximately $402 each week, and it's only this amount which will be used for tax deductions regardless of which loan you choose to take out.

There are some risks in the interest-only option as well as some benefits, so you will need to make your decision about which loan would ideally suit you.

Disadvantages of an interest-only loan include

- Making no headway in the amount that you have borrowed, so no equity is building up from your repayments. Basically if your mortgage starts at $250,000, it will still be $250,000 when it comes time to sell.

- The property may not increase in value by the time you decide to sell, which will mean that you have made no money or built up any equity for the duration of the loan.

- They are not a long-term option; you can generally only take out an interest only loan for up to five or seven years. After that you will have to reapply or take on the full principal plus interest repayments.

The benefits of an interest-only loan are

- It can provide you with more control over your cash-flow;
- You will have reduced monthly mortgage repayments; and
- You will have the ability to purchase a more expensive property.

There can be quite a significant difference in repayments, and which type of loan you take out could be the distinction between a positively geared property and a negatively geared one. With the interest-only option, the principal amount will be paid out at the time that you sell the property; until then, you may wish to enjoy the lower repayment option that the interest-only loan gives you. Your capital growth will be achieved from the sale of the property in the long term. Ultimately, the decision on what type of loan you get is entirely up to you and should work in line with your financial goals.

Chapter 9

DO! KEEP THOROUGH RECORDS

I have mentioned that there are various tax benefits available to you as an investor, but the only way for you to maximise these benefits is (as boring as it sounds) by keeping meticulous records. You need to keep all your receipts, tax invoices, and bank statements as organised as possible throughout the financial year.

On the following page, I have provided a table that will be useful to you in understanding the various types of financial records that you will need to keep and also the items that your accountant will be reviewing at tax time.

Depreciation is also listed, so be sure that you have the relevant schedule completed by a quantity surveyor as soon as you purchase your investment property or when any improvements are made.

RENTAL WORKSHEET

Income

Rental income	
Other rental related income	
Gross rent	$

Expenses

Interest on loan/s	
Borrowing charges	
Council rates	
Land tax	
Water charges	
Legal expenses	
Real estate fees and charges	
Advertising costs	
Body corporate fees and charges	
Repairs & maintenance	
Yard maintenance	
Cleaning	
Pest control	
Insurance (landlord and property)	
Travel	
Stationery, telephone & postage	
Sundry	
Capital works deductions (building costs)	
Depreciation (wear and tear)	
Total Expenses	$

Net Rental Income or Loss
(Gross rent *less* total expenses)

$_____

As you can see, there are a wide variety of taxable deductions that you can offset against your rental income. The table is by no means exhaustive, and available deductions will vary with each country, but it does cover the majority of costs that are associated with owning an investment property.

Even if you are a naturally disorganised person, I urge you to, at the very least, have a folder allocated for each individual property that you hold where you can keep the documents relevant for that particular financial year. It will make both your workload and your accountant's workload a lot less chaotic come tax time.

Chapter 10

DON'T! USE ONLY ONE LENDER

The reality is that you wouldn't want only one bank or lender having the final say about when you can and cannot borrow money, how and when you can grow your portfolio, or even what you can and cannot do with your own assets. So it should also be important to you that you use a range of lenders for your different property investments or projects.

The main benefit of using a variety of lenders is that you are not risking the possibility of *one* lender, who holds all your mortgages, suddenly going into receivership or changing its lending policy so that it no longer applies to your particular properties or your personal circumstances. If this happens, you could be facing a massive refinance, and if it's seventeen properties that you hold with this one bank, a refinance will be no easy feat.

> *Spreading the mortgages among different lenders*
>
> *= minimising the risk.*

To be investing successfully, you should, ideally, be using other people's money; you must also make sure that those *other* people are also *different* people wherever possible.

Additionally, each property should have its own mortgage. The complications involved at the end of the financial year in dividing one mortgage among several properties are both time-consuming and messy for you and your accountant. You would much prefer that your tax specialist spends that time checking and rechecking that every available tax benefit is claimed rather than sifting through paperwork to identify the value of each property, calculating the interest portion of your mortgage repayments, and allocating the correct rental income to it.

If your personal goals are bigger than simply acquiring properties and doing basic short-term capital growth strategies, and you are aiming to become a property developer (i.e. where you buy a large portion of land, subdivide it into several blocks, and build a number of residential properties), then an option worth considering when seeking finance is an 'angel investor'.

While you invest with other people's money, your money should be invested in your education on investment strategies. Once you have a clear understanding on the ins and outs of investing successfully, you will be ready to tackle your first project and target your first investor. Whether it is a major bank or an angel investor, you will need to understand what you are talking about when it comes to investing.

> *If you can't explain it simply,*
>
> *You don't understand it well enough*
>
> Albert Einstein

You will also need to present it well to those that are financing your investment, and that means you need to train your brain to think, work, and play as an investor would.

It is worth knowing a little more about angel investors if you are hoping to develop properties. Originally, the word 'angel' in investment was limited to those who provided funds for Broadway productions. Nowadays, it essentially refers to a person who is prepared to lend their personal funds to help budding entrepreneurs start their business in any type of venture, including property development.

Many business ventures are funded by angel investors as opposed to traditional banks, and there are some significant advantages to angel investing. For example, an angel investor can provide you with

1) **Important contacts.** This is something that will become the driving force behind your business's success. You need to know people, whether it's a builder, a project manager, or another potential investor. Contacts are invaluable to you as a business owner.

2) **Knowledge and education.** Your business cannot thrive without a thorough understanding of what it is that you, yourself, have to offer. While it may be apparent in your mind, a lot of people will have difficulty getting the message across clearly. Often, angel investors that will be interested in your business venture will have also had experience in the real estate property and development industry, and they will be more than happy to share that information with you.

3) **Support.** Unlike a traditional bank that will hand over the funds and leave you to your own devices, angel investors can offer you mentoring to help keep you heading in the right direction on your path to success.

To find an angel investor, it's as simple as going online and typing 'angel investor' and your country into your Internet search engine; then you will be supplied with a variety of networks that can help you connect with an investor for your project.

These angel investment networks are designed to help the entrepreneur (you) connect with an investor (other people's money). You will need to construct a proposal or business plan and submit it to the online angel investment agency. They will then forward your information and business proposal to potential investors that they find suitable; any interested investors will notify the company and—voila! You have just met other people's money.

If you have done your homework on property investment strategies and also on the locations that you are looking to commence your project, then you will be more than capable of constructing a viable and realistic business plan that will capture the attention of your lender or angel investor. Your education and you gaining an understanding of the subject is so important; it will help you clarify your goals and promote your idea.

You need to *connect* with those that can potentially fund your investment. To successfully make the connection, you should understand and appreciate the mind of an investor and what is and what is not important to them. All the information and assistance is out there just waiting for you to grab and use, so get to it!

Chapter 11

DO! PAY THE PROFESSIONALS

This topic is short and sweet; pay the professionals to do their job, while you do yours.

You will need qualified accountants (to supply you important tax information, to file your returns, to create your companies or trusts), conveyancers or settlement agents (to facilitate the settlement of your properties), lawyers (to advise you about your obligations and ensure the legal process is adhered to), and so on and so forth.

More importantly, you will need to determine that they are reputable in their respective fields. Your neighbour may tell you that their financial planner is 'the best', but that is only in their opinion and opinions are subjective. Seek an objective view, research their credentials, read testimonials and reviews, then meet with them and decide whether these are people that you want to use as a part of your team, dealing with them on a regular basis. If they're not, move on to the next one.

Ask for their experience, ask questions about their knowledge in real estate investing, and ensure that they know what they are talking about without having to 'get back to you on that'. After all, it is your wealth, your assets, and your future that is being handled by them. If they look after you and your goals, you will have no problem in paying them what they are worth for their expertise.

The only item that I, wholeheartedly, believe that you should complete yourself is your business plan. Please do not employ someone to do this. It seems like the easy way out because, let's face it, they *are* hard to do, but there are business plan templates online to help you get started.

The reason that I believe that you should do the business plan without outside sources is because I, personally, have created many a business plan for people over the years, and, in my experience, those that I had prepared it for, simply viewed it as more pieces of paper to add to the business pile. They did read it, they did seem happy with it, but they didn't see it as an intensive strategy method towards their business's success; it was just more reading material. They hadn't put their mind, their heart or their soul into it.

You are the manager, the planner, the researcher, and the record-keeper of your investment portfolio. These are the things that you need to do well.

Pay the professionals for the jobs that they do; your time is better spent setting your goals, seeking your next viable investment property, and increasing your knowledge on successful investment strategies; not in educating yourself about the conveyancing process, studying accounting, or getting a law degree in your spare time.

Chapter 12

DON'T! DELAY, START SAVING NOW

By now, hopefully you have an idea of where you are heading and also the basic strategies that you need to implement in order to put those ideas into practice.

The truth is that the vast majority of people *do* need some savings in their bank account before getting started. Even though I have explained that you will primarily be using other people's money to invest with, you will inevitably need some of your own funds available at the outset. Traditional banks and lenders would like to see your savings in order for you to get off the ground, and they aren't terribly flexible in this regard.

Sure, a lot of real estate tycoons will tell you that you can, in fact, start with nothing, and while I do have some faith in their words of wisdom, I would also take the opportunity to point out that unless you are an exceptional salesperson and can convince someone to sell you their property with no money down, or that vendor finance is the way of the future, or even to offer them an option for a potential purchase in two years' time, then the 'no money down' strategy may not work so effectively for you, and you will find that you will have some difficulty starting up without any funds in your account.

Whether your 'goal' account is for the highly demanded 'savings' for a deposit, or to set up your company, or even just to be able to jump on a plane when a great investment property hits the market on the other side of the country, if you have no savings at this point, it's time to start *now!*

First and foremost, you need to remember and recognise how important your goal is to you and how important you are to your business. Run your home as though you are running a business, a business that will be successful. It has its set targets, and you are the driving force in making the decisions that will help you reach your business goals.

In a household, budgets can go awry the second an excessive electricity bill arrives, a school camp is announced, or an unexpected and costly emergency crops up. But that's okay; it will still be manageable as long as you stick to some key rules. So in keeping it brief and relatively simple, the steps that you may want to consider for getting some initial savings together are as follows:

1) Pay yourself first

This is easier said than done, but for all intents and purposes, it *is* a necessity; after all, you need to sacrifice to reach your goal, and lenders are demanding more and more loan prerequisites each year. You are expected to pay your rent (or your current mortgage), save just as much, and also have a nice car parked in your garage.

If you meet those criteria, good for you; if not, you will probably have to find a good mortgage broker to help you jump through the hoops that lenders will set in your way.

Run your home as you would run a business, visualise yourself as the chief executive officer, and how many CEOs do you know that will work for free? Exactly, there are none.

Have your high interest savings account (or goal account) where, before any other bills are paid, you are paid. Whether it's $50, $100, or $200 each week—pay *you* first. Regardless of the amount of money that you are putting away, it is proof to the lender that you are capable of saving in case any unforeseen expenses occur in the future, affecting your ability to repay your mortgage with them.

2) Give up the junk food and drinks

You know the ones: just a quick drive through after the grocery shopping (which probably cost more than you budgeted for because you went shopping while you were hungry), the 'I don't feel like cooking' takeaway, and the chocolate bar you picked up when you ran into the store to *just* grab some bread and milk.

The simplest but sometimes hardest way to save money is to *think* before you spend; *think* before you pick up the phone and order that pizza. *Think;* how much will it cost? *Think;* it will probably cost $30, and then $3 in the fuel to get there. Then *think;* what is my goal? Is the pizza worth delaying the goal? Probably not. So make the time to get up and go and cook dinner; then take the money that you were going to spend on the takeout, and place it in your savings, even if it is just a temporary jar under the kitchen bench until you get to the bank. Physically place that $33 into your goal account.

Feel like a $2.50 soft drink? Put that $2.50 into your goal account. Want a packet of salt and vinegar chips? Put that money into your goal. And so on and so forth. You will be surprised how quickly funds accumulate in your savings; only now you have something to show for the money that has an incredible talent of disappearing from your wallet—*a bank balance.*

It is also important that the money that you place in here is over and above your 'pay yourself first' savings.

3) Save that additional money

Without a doubt the majority of households will receive extra money throughout the year, often by way of a tax return, and sometimes by selling items in a garage sale. Some people can gain by applying for an advance or receiving a bonus. *Use* it, put it straight into your goal account; you have lived without it so far. What makes you need it so desperately now?

So put it into your goal account. Similarly, it is savings that is above and beyond your 'pay yourself first' and 'give up the junk' savings.

~

Your goal is paramount, not a new CD player for the car, not fish and chips for dinner, and not a new pair of shoes for Saturday night—they can all come later, when you have achieved your first goal. The rest of your household budget can and will work around these three simple steps, if you let it.

> - *Pay yourself first;*
> - *Give up the junk; and*
> - *Stash away that extra cash.*

Imagine how quickly your money will accumulate by doing these three simple savings each and every week! You will be well on your way to reaching your goals.

CONCLUSION

So there you have it, the simple version of both the potential value in the property market as well as the possible pitfalls, and how they can be avoided—the dos and don'ts of real estate investing.

Property investment can be a very rewarding business; the key is to approach it as a business, not as a hobby. When you approach it as a business, you will be more inclined to ensure its success, research ways to grow your wealth, and protect yourself from any losses.

Throughout this book, I have taken you through the advantages arising from positive gearing, short-term capital growth, researching each property thoroughly, protecting your investments, and maximising your tax benefits. Let's take a moment to recap.

Positive gearing. You should now be aware of the key difference between negative gearing and positive gearing and why it is important that your properties give you an income rather than cost you money.

Positive Gearing = Asset

Negative Gearing = Liability

Short-term capital growth. We discussed short-term capital growth and how you can create more equity in your properties. Equity is the most important consideration when creating and growing your portfolio. Seek properties that can help you create wealth almost immediately rather than simply waiting for the medium—to long-term growth in its value.

Ways to *create* equity:

- Build
- Renovate
- Extend
- Subdivide

Research. Even though it is time-consuming and can be quite tedious, it is an important form of protecting yourself.

> *Researching = Reducing the risk*

At the end of this book, I have provided a checklist for you; I encourage you to photocopy it, keep it in a handy place, and use it each and every time that you are looking at a potential investment property to add to your portfolio.

Asset protection. Simply put, there is absolutely no point in investing in real estate if you are not protecting it to the best of your ability. There are so many scenarios that can put you in a position where you stand to lose everything that you have worked for; which is why it is imperative that you do everything possible to stop that from occurring.

Ways to protect yourself *and* your assets:

- Complete your contract correctly.
- Be insured and *know* your policies back to front.
- Establish a company or trust to hold your assets.
- Pay your taxes.
- Use different lenders.
- Pay the professionals.

Maximise tax benefits. It is important to maximise your tax benefits; it may be the difference between a negatively geared property and a positively geared one.

Be sure to

- keep all your receipts and records together;
- hold individual mortgages for each property; and

- obtain a depreciation schedule for each asset.

~

With that, I hope that you have enjoyed reading this book, and the information that I have provided you. Follow these simple steps, and you should be well on your way to successful investing when it comes to real estate.

I take this opportunity to wish you well with your current and your future goals for your investment portfolio.

YOUR CHECKLIST

PROPERTY ADDRESS: _____

LISTED PRICE: $ _____ **OFFER:** $ _____

Before I Make an Offer:

Have I done the maths?	Yes ☐	No ☐
Weekly mortgage repayment amount?	$ _____	
Estimated weekly rental income?	$ _____	
What is the balance?	$ _____	
Is it a positively geared property?	Yes ☐	No ☐
Short-term capital growth potential?	Yes ☐	No ☐
How? Building ☐ Renovating ☐ Extending ☐	Subdividing ☐	
Have I confirmed this with the local council?	Yes ☐	No ☐
Have I done the local area research?	Yes ☐	No ☐
What is the population? Increased ☐	Declined ☐	
Nearest school?	_____ km	
Does the school have a good reputation?	Yes ☐	No ☐
Recent or planned developments in the area?	Yes ☐	No ☐
Nearest public transport?	_____ km	
Nearest airport? _____ km or	n/a (rural) ☐	
Is this a high crime rate area?	Yes ☐	No ☐

NOTES:

_____
_____
_____
_____
_____
_____
_____

Under Contract

Have I specified my finance lender on contract?	Yes ☐	No ☐
Due diligence clause added to contract?	Yes ☐	No ☐
Building and pest inspections organised?	Yes ☐ No ☐	n/a ☐

NOTES:

_____
_____
_____
_____
_____
_____
_____
_____
_____
_____

After Settlement

Tax depreciation schedule organised?	Yes ☐	No ☐

NOTES:

_____
_____
_____
_____
_____
_____
_____
_____
_____
_____

INDEX

A

Accountants 9, 39-42, 51, 56, 59
angel investors 56-7
asset protection 33, 37, 39, 43, 66
assets xi, 3, 5, 9, 11, 18, 31, 33-4, 39-40, 42, 45-7, 55, 59, 65-7
Australia 12, 25
Australian Bureau of Statistics 25

B

bank, traditional 57, 61
bank account 5, 7, 9, 61
beneficiary 40, 42
business 25, 42-3, 56-7, 62, 65
business plan 57, 59-60
business structures 41-2

C

capital growth 6, 11-13, 15, 17-18, 20-2, 24-5, 27, 46, 49, 56, 65, 68
cash flow 9, 21
caveat Emptor 27
Community titling 16
company 16, 33-4, 39-43, 57, 59, 61, 66
company titling 16
contract 17, 27-8, 30-1, 34, 66, 69

conveyancers 59
crime rates 25

D

damage v, 29, 34-5, 41
debts 36-7
deductions 3, 12, 15, 41, 47-8, 52-3
depreciation 8, 12, 47-8, 51-2, 67, 69
Discretionary Family Trust 40
due diligence 25, 30

E

education 56-7
equity 3-4, 12, 15, 17, 45-6, 48, 65-6
expenses 8-9, 52, 62

F

failure 19
fear 19, 21

G

gearing
  negative 5-9, 65
  positive 5-6, 65
goal account 62-3

H

house 8, 14, 19-20, 45-6
Hybrid Trust 40

I

income v, 5-6, 8-11, 20, 23, 36, 40, 52, 65
  passive 5-6, 9-10, 20, 37
  personal 5-6, 40-1
income tax 5-6, 9, 40
inspection 28-30
insurance 26, 33-7, 43, 52
  income protection 36
  landlord 34-5
  life 36
insurance companies 33-4, 36
insurance policy 33-4
interest-only loan 8, 48-9
Internet 23-5, 57
investments v, 1, 3-4, 6, 8-9, 12, 15, 23-6, 33, 36, 39-42, 45-8, 55-8, 60-1, 65-7
investors 5, 21, 47

L

land 16-17, 24, 28, 45-6, 52, 56
landlord 34-5, 52
laws 27, 39, 41
lenders 9, 28, 36, 55, 57, 61-2, 66
lending institution 28
liability v, 5, 7, 10, 31, 39-41, 65
loan 6, 8-9, 28, 34, 36, 48-9
local council 16-17, 24, 31, 46, 68

M

money 3, 5-6, 9-10, 15, 23, 28-30, 36, 45, 47-8, 56, 61-5
mortgage 3, 6-10, 20-1, 28, 30, 48-9, 55-6, 62, 66, 68
mortgage calculator 6
mortgage repayments 6-10, 20-1, 56

N

negative gearing calculators 8

P

pest inspection 28-31, 69
population 23-5, 68
portfolio
  investment 19, 60, 67
  property 3, 36-7, 47
professionals 59-60, 66
profit 6, 8, 11-12, 17, 20, 40, 45-7
property
  negatively geared 5-8, 66
  positively geared 6-7, 12-13, 17-18, 28, 31, 39, 49, 68
property investment 12, 47, 55, 65
property market 3, 21, 65
public transport 24, 68

R

real estate v, 1, 3-6, 9, 11-12, 17, 21, 23, 25, 27, 33, 35, 39-43, 47, 65-7
Real estate agents 17, 23, 45
Real Estate Investing 1, 3-4, 17, 33, 42, 47, 59, 65
real estate investors 12, 39, 47
real estate market 6, 11-12, 17, 21
renovating 13, 15, 17, 31
rental 9, 17, 20, 24, 35, 52
rental income 6, 8-9, 45-6, 52-3, 56, 68
rental return 7-8, 12, 15, 20-1, 25
research 10, 15, 20, 22-7, 30, 34, 46, 59-60, 66, 68
risk 19-22, 26, 39, 41, 48, 55, 66

S

savings 61-4
scarcity 24
schools 24, 68
settlement agents 59

short-term capital growth 11-13, 15, 17, 20, 46, 56, 65, 68
strata-titling 16, 20
subdivision 16-17, 30, 46
suburbs 23-5, 31

T

tax benefits 5, 8-9, 13, 21, 41, 47-8, 51, 56, 65-6
tax deductions 8, 47-8
Tax Office 12, 47
tax planning 40
tax specialists 9, 40, 56
taxable deductions 40, 53
taxation v, 8, 39-41, 47
taxes 12, 41, 45, 66
tenants 25, 34-5
termites 29
trustee 40, 42
trusts 39-43, 59, 66

U

Unit Trust 40

W

wealth xi, 3, 12, 23, 45, 59, 65

ABOUT THE AUTHOR

S. M. Cullen has owned and operated businesses for over fifteen years. She holds an Associate Degree in Law from *Southern Cross University*, NSW, which led her into the legal field of conveyancing and settlements.

These roles sparked an interest in investing in property, and she went on to study the subject further. During this journey, she realised that there had to be an easier and more straightforward way to get the message across, and so was born *Keeping it Simple—the Dos and Don'ts of Real Estate Investing*.

www.ingramcontent.com/pod-product-compliance
Lightning Source LLC
Chambersburg PA
CBHW021003180526
45163CB00005B/1881